W9-BWT-807

JOBS IN THE
U.S. SPACE
FORCE

KATHLEEN A. KLATTE

ROSEN
PUBLISHING

NEW YORK

Published in 2023 by The Rosen Publishing Group, Inc.
29 East 21st Street, New York, NY 10010

Copyright © 2023 by The Rosen Publishing Group, Inc.

First Edition

Cataloging-in-Publication Data

Names: Klatte, Kathleen A.
Title: Jobs in the U.S. Space Force / Kathleen A Klatte.
Description: New York : Rosen Publishing, 2023. | Series: Exploring military careers | Includes glossary and index.
Identifiers: ISBN 9781499472332 (pbk.) | ISBN 9781499472349 (library bound) | ISBN 9781499472356 (ebook)
Subjects: LCSH: United States. Space Force--Juvenile literature. | United States. Department of Defense--Juvenile literature. | Outer space--Juvenile literature.
Classification: LCC UG1515.K53 2023 | DDC 358'.8--dc23

Some of the images in this book illustrate individuals who are models. The depictions do not imply actual situations or events.

Manufactured in the United States of America

CPSIA Compliance Information: Batch #CSRYA23. For further information, contact Rosen Publishing, New York, New York, at 1-800-237-9932.

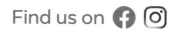

CONTENTS

CHAPTER 1

THE U.S. SPACE FORCE

Everyone knows the stories and legends of the minutemen and colonial militia during the American Revolution. However, by the mid-18th century, most nations maintained professional armies and navies. If the American colonies were to have any chance at becoming a secure, sovereign nation, they would need armed forces of their own. So, on June 14, 1775—even before the Declaration of Independence was written—the Continental Congress formed the Continental Army.

Alan Shepard was the first American in space. Anyone with the "right stuff" to follow In hls footsteps can find an exciting career in the U.S. Space Force.

The concepts of fighting sea vessels and soldiers trained to fight on ships or on land were well understood at the time. The U.S. Navy and Marine Corps were also established in 1775. In 1789, the new U.S. Congress created the Department of War—part of the executive branch of the government—to oversee the armed forces. The precursor of the modern Coast Guard was created in 1790. Service academies to train officers were established, beginning with the United States Military Academy at West Point in 1802.

Over time, the U.S. military has adapted to evolving technology. On land, horses gave way to motor vehicles and eventually armored tanks. At sea, wooden-hulled sailing ships were replaced by ironclad steamships and submarines. Still, these were evolutions of fighting on land and sea, which were familiar battlegrounds after decades of war.

At the beginning of the 20th century, an entirely new dimension was introduced: flight. The Wright brothers' first flight occurred in 1903, and in 1907, the U.S. Army organized the Aeronautical Division to take charge of military applications of flight with balloons, planes, and other early aircraft. In 1910, the U.S. Navy began investigating the possibility of launching aircraft from ships. The navy's initial interest in aviation would eventually result in today's enormous nuclear-powered aircraft carriers, which carry a crew of thousands and have the ability to launch and land jet aircraft. The army's flight program would become the Army Air Corps, which would eventually become the United States Air Force.

In 1947, the U.S. Air Force was created as a separate branch of the military to take charge of air combat operations. The U.S. Air Force Academy was founded in 1954. During the 1950s and 1960s, the U.S. Air Force conducted extensive testing to create aircraft that could travel faster than the speed of sound.

Over time, the domain of the air began to include space. The air force was involved in research to create a reusable "space plane." Long-range missiles became worldwide weapons during the Cold War, and there was an increased reliance on satellites for communications and intelligence gathering. In 1982, the Air Force Space Command was created to unify military space operations. In 2005, its operations expanded to include yet another new realm: cyberspace.

By the beginning of the 21st century, space operations had expanded to include civilian as well as military and government projects and assets. Many functions critical to civilian life depend on assets in space and the flow of information through cyberspace. As a result, it was decided that a new, separate branch of the military was needed.

AIR FORCE SPACE COMMAND

The Air Force Space Command (AFSPC) was established in 1982. It was headquartered at Peterson AFB in Colorado. AFSPC had command and control of all Department of Defense satellites. In addition, it monitored radar and satellite early warning systems in case of a long-range missile attack.

In 1991, AFSPC provided support for other branches of the military involved in Operation Desert Storm. Following the 9/11 terrorist attacks, AFSPC provided intelligence and other data to aid in troop deployments and attack plans. Satellites were used to gather weather information

(continued on the next page)

(continued from the previous page)

and topographical data to help determine the best timing and placement of ground troops and assets. Keyhole satellite images were also used to see where enemy troops and weapons were placed.

AFSPC's scope expanded to include cyberspace in 2005. The military has always required security in its communications. Battle plans, troop movements, and state secrets have always needed to be protected. However, now the orderly function of civilian society also depends on cybersecurity. Banking, communications, and daily commercial activity all rely on satellites and the internet.

As of 2019, the AFSPC has become the core of the new U.S. Space Force. Its mission is to protect and defend U.S. interests in both space and cyberspace.

A NEW MODERN BRANCH

The United States Space Force (USSF) is the newest branch of the armed services. It was formed on December 20, 2019, as part of the National Defense Authorization Act and was signed into law by President Donald Trump. It is the first new branch of the armed forces to be established in 73 years. Many young people have big dreams of working in the United States' space program. Many also feel a call to protect and defend their country. For these young people, the USSF is a dream come true.

The first chief of space operations was General Jay Raymond. He was appointed by the president. The first senior enlisted adviser was Chief Master Sergeant Roger Towberman. The USSF is headquartered in the Pentagon, along with the other branches of the armed forces. When the USSF was established, some air force bases—including Vandenberg Air Force Base—were redesignated as Space Command Bases. The USSF was given an operating budget of about $17 billion.

Each branch of the U.S. armed forces has its own distinctive symbol. The symbol of the USSF is called the Delta. It is a design that looks something like an arrowhead. The outer edge is silver, symbolizing protection. The inside is black to symbolize space. Two spires represent a rocket launching. Four segments symbolize the U.S. Army, Navy, Air Force, and Marine Corps working together to protect space. In the center is the star Polaris, symbolizing the core values that drive the USSF.

The design for the U.S. Space Force official seal was approved by President Trump in January 2020. The motto of the USSF is Semper Supra, Latin for "Always Above." The Delta appears on the USSF flag with the date 2019 in Roman numerals, reflecting the year that the USSF was established.

The USSF was formed from the Air Force Space Command (AFSPC), which was initially tasked with deploying and monitoring satellite activity. Its scope expanded to include command and control of America's nuclear missile arsenal and cyberspace security.

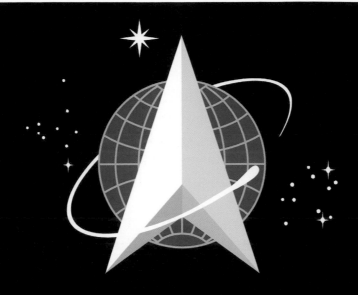

UNITED STATES SPACE FORCE

M M X I X

This is the flag of the United States Space Force. It is dated 2019, the year the USSF was officially established.

Initially, 16,000 personnel were transferred from the Air Force Space Command to the USSF. The young USSF remains associated with the air force, similar to the Marine Corps's affiliation with the navy.

For centuries, the United States' armed forces have defended the nation with distinction, first on land and sea, and later in the air. Now the United States faces a new challenge—defending U.S. interests in space. Though alien invaders are still firmly in the realm of science fiction, American communications and defense rely on satellites that orbit Earth.

Protecting these satellites is a key part of preserving modern society. Think what might happen if there were suddenly no television broadcasts or phone communication. What if there were no GPS navigation systems? What if Wall Street's computer systems stopped working? The chaos would be unimaginable.

The modern world relies on satellite technology for nearly everything, from using the internet to buying groceries.

The USSF also protects cyberspace. Think of all the industries that use data gathered by satellites and communicated via the internet. Banking and commerce depend on the internet. So does the travel industry. Schools around the country depend on computer-generated weather forecasts to determine if it is safe to open.

As much as U.S. leaders might hope that space exploration would be free from conflict, the fact is that other nations have a presence in space now. Some of those nations, such as China and North Korea, are historically unfriendly toward the United States. The USSF's mission includes monitoring for the threat of a long-range missile attack, as well as maintaining U.S. missile defenses and countermeasures.

Currently, the USSF is divided into three major commands:

- Space Operations Command (SPOC)
- Space Systems Command
- Space Training and Readiness Command (STARCOM)

SPOC is responsible for providing intelligence, secure cyber operations, and combat support for USSF missions, as well as projects with partner agencies.

Space Systems Command's mission is to develop and deliver the technology needed to keep space and cyberspace secure.

STARCOM is the USSF's center for education and training. In 2021, the first class of enlisted intelligence specialists graduated from courses at STARCOM.

The USSF is still defining itself, but there is already a range of career opportunities involving cutting-edge technology. Opportunities include:

- Maintaining satellites
- Monitoring missile systems
- Working cybersecurity
- Conducting cyberwarfare

The USSF also offers variations of more traditional military careers, such as:

- Intelligence
- Engineering
- Acquisitions

Members of the USSF have many similar ambitions and interests. They dream about one day flying in space to see what exists beyond Earth. They want to solve complicated puzzles and find the answers to difficult questions. They get to use fascinating cutting-edge technology. Perhaps more than anything, members of the USSF are part of a strong team with a shared goal.

There are many exciting career paths available in the USSF. Young people with a keen interest in science, technology, engineering, or mathematics (STEM) and a desire to serve their country may increasingly find that a career in the USSF is the right option for them.

NASA

The National Aeronautics and Space Administration (NASA) is the U.S.'s civil space program. It was formed in 1958 from the National Advisory Committee for Aeronautics (NACA). NASA is the organization that sent the first Americans into space and the first humans to the moon. It is the leader in Mars exploration. NASA maintains the only national laboratory in space. Besides studying outer space, NASA satellites also study Earth, gathering and evaluating valuable information about climate change and weather patterns.

Although astronauts are the most public faces associated with NASA, the agency has 20 facilities across the country and generates more than 312,000 jobs. The technology needed to achieve its scientific goals often has to be created, offering many opportunities for engineers and computer programmers. Advanced remote-controlled robotic devices have been particularly useful for exploring Mars. NASA also employs educators, both to make its research accessible to the general public and to get the next generation of explorers excited about STEM studies.

Although segregation was still legal in the early days of the space program, NASA tended to be more progressive than other organizations. It believed that the magnitude of the task it had undertaken demanded the finest minds available, regardless of race. One of those minds belonged to an African American woman named Katherine Johnson (1918–2020), who helped compute the trajectories for many early space flights by hand. In 2015, President Obama awarded her the Presidential Medal of Freedom, and in 2016, NASA named a building in her honor.

NASA is a civilian agency, so it does not work directly with missile systems, but it does have a space flight program. Becoming an astronaut is extremely competitive, and NASA has its pick of fully qualified individuals. Although there is training provided once an applicant is selected for the program, NASA doesn't have a service academy or programs to defray college expenses, like the military. In order to be considered to work at NASA, you must already have achieved at least one college degree.

NASA's Vehicle Assembly Building (VAB) boasts the largest set of doors in the world! They're 465 feet (142 m) high and take 45 minutes to open or close.

CHAPTER 2

AMERICA IN SPACE

Space is a physical place. It exists beyond Earth's atmosphere. Physical objects, like spacecraft, rockets, or missiles, can move through space. Objects like space stations and satellites can be placed there. People can live and work in space and even move around outside of a vehicle if they have the proper equipment.

Of course, any object that can exist in space can be damaged or destroyed by another object. Sometimes this is accidental—a meteorite or some man-made debris can collide with another object, causing considerable damage. Damage can also be caused deliberately, with missiles. One of the USSF's primary objectives is to protect America's assets—the physical objects—that have been placed in space or that move through space, and of course, the people that live and work there.

THE SPACE RACE

Along with Russia, the U.S. has been one of the leaders in space exploration for decades. The first man-made satellite was launched by the Soviet Union. The first human in space, Yuri Gagarin, was Soviet. American spacecraft were the first to land on the moon, and American citizens were the first humans to walk there. The first reusable manned spacecraft—the space shuttle—was American. So was the first spacecraft to land on Mars.

Though other nations have sent unmanned probe vehicles to the moon, the U.S. remains the only country to have landed humans on the moon and returned them safely to Earth.

Where the U.S. has led, other nations have followed. China, Japan, the European Space Agency, and now India have sent unmanned spacecraft to the moon. In 2020, China became the second nation to land a rover on Mars. As with any other form of exploration, it is not enough to just be the first to get there. The USSF exists to protect both the United States' physical interests in space and the information that moves through cyberspace.

FAMOUS FIRSTS

1947	First living things intentionally sent into space—fruit flies aboard a V-2 rocket (U.S.)
1957	First man-made satellite launched (Sputnik, USSR)
1961	First human in space (Yuri Gagarin, USSR)
1965	First Mars fly-by (Mariner 4, U.S.)
1969	First moon landing (Apollo 11, U.S.)
1971	First manned space station (Salyut 1, USSR)
1976	First successful Mars landing (*Viking 1*, U.S.)
1981	First reusable spacecraft (space shuttle, U.S.)

WHY A SPACE MILITARY?

There is a plaque on the moon that reads: "Here men from the planet earth first set foot on the moon—July 1969 A.D.—We came in peace for all mankind." So why is there now a need for a branch of the military for peaceful exploration? The fact is that space exploration missions have always drawn from the ranks of the military. The scientists who designed the rockets that catapulted satellites and space capsules into orbit started out designing bombs and missiles for warfare. The first astronauts were recruited from the ranks of air force test pilots and naval aviators.

This is the last of six plaques that U.S. astronauts left on the moon.

To date, the Naval Academy has produced the most NASA astronauts, followed by the Air Force Academy. The original astronaut candidates had backgrounds in aviation and engineering. They had to be shorter than 5 feet 9 inches (175 cm) to fit inside the Mercury space capsule. They were also required to have a college degree.

For every step of humanity's journey into space, people have asked questions like "Why do we need to do this?" and "Aren't there better uses for our tax dollars?" Looking around at some of the ongoing problems right here on Earth, those can seem like reasonable questions. The answers to these challenges have varied over time.

Since the earliest civilizations, people have looked to the stars in wonder and dreamed about what might be out there. Throughout the centuries, the development of bigger and better telescopes offered the chance to see farther out into the sky and apply scientific reasoning to each new object that became visible.

It was not until the mid-20th century that the science and technology existed to actually propel objects into orbit around Earth. Technology that had been used to deadly effect in World War II was refocused on exploring space. Both the U.S. and the Soviet Union recruited former Nazi scientists and engineers for their young space programs. While many people hoped that exploration would be peaceful, there was always the fear of what might happen if a hostile nation established a foothold in space before the United States.

Peenemünde, Germany, was the site of research and production of the V-2 rocket. The site was bombed by the Royal Air Force in 1943.

OPERATION PAPERCLIP

During World War II, German scientists made tremendous advances in rocket technology. The U.S. and the USSR were both eager to continue this research. Operation Paperclip was a project of the Joint Intelligence Objectives Agency (JIOA), which brought about 1,600 scientists and engineers, as well as their families, to the United States.

President Truman sanctioned the program but forbade the recruitment of actual Nazis. However, intelligence operatives felt that their information was too valuable to lose—or worse, fall into communist hands—and records were rewritten as needed.

The most notable among the German scientists was Wernher von Braun (1912–1977), who developed the V-2 rocket for the Third Reich. He would go on to head the U.S. Saturn rocket project. Although many people now consider him to be a war criminal, his knowledge was crucial to the space race. Von Braun was a gifted speaker, and he even produced a program with Walt Disney to promote the idea of landing men on the moon.

The motion pictures *The Right Stuff*, *Hidden Figures*, and *Apollo 13* all depict German scientists and technicians who worked to make manned spaceflight a reality.

One of the earliest and strongest proponents of America's space program was President Lyndon Johnson. As Senate majority leader during President Dwight Eisenhower's administration, Johnson worked to secure funding and support for the program. He was wise enough to realize that the research and technology needed for space exploration would also benefit the civilian job market and economy.

He led investigations into how the Soviet Sputnik program got ahead of the United States' early efforts to launch a satellite. Johnson was instrumental in the creation of NASA from the National Advisory Committee for Aeronautics (NACA).

As president, Johnson continued President John F. Kennedy's legacy of space projects. His administration introduced the Outer Space Treaty (OST), which prohibited the introduction of nuclear weapons into space and the claiming of celestial objects for any one country. The treaty was signed by the United States, Great Britain, and the Soviet Union. It was hoped that it would lead to peaceful and cooperative space exploration.

In order to raise public support for the space program—and the money it cost—astronauts have always been involved in public relations. John Glenn, the clean-cut marine war hero and first American to orbit Earth, was a particular public favorite. Decades later, so was Christa McAuliffe, the first civilian to fly in space. Members of the cast of the television show *Star Trek* have also been involved in publicity and recruitment campaigns for the space program. The show presented a vision of a peaceful, united planet that many hoped would carry over into real-life space exploration.

During the 1950s and 1960s, the goal was to launch satellites—and later manned flights—into space before the communist Soviet Union. More than 60 years later, the Cold War is over. Why is the military headed into space today? The answer is

The cast of *Star Trek*, shown here in 1976, helped make the United States' space programs popular around the country.

that the nations of the world are never fully at peace. The United States is not the only country with space flight and missile capability. The entire global communications network runs off of orbiting satellites. Protecting those satellites and the information they channel is vital to preserving modern life.

The USSF is also responsible for protecting the United States from a missile attack by a hostile nation. It maintains and operates the systems that

The prototype space shuttle was named *Enterprise* following a letter-writing campaign from *Star Trek* fans. In addition, cast members from the original series participated in recruiting and publicity for NASA.

monitor for incoming enemy missiles, as well as the U.S. arsenal of intercontinental ballistic missiles (ICBMs). These are land-based missiles that carry a nuclear warhead. They have a range of 3,500 miles (5,632 km). Russia and China have similar missiles.

THE RIGHT STUFF

The first U.S. astronauts were recruited from the ranks of air force test pilots and naval aviators. The original pool of astronaut candidates had to meet certain height requirements to ensure that they'd fit inside the proposed design for the Mercury space capsule. They were also required to be college graduates. They were subjected to a battery of intense physical tests and medical procedures to try to determine if they would be able to survive the extreme conditions in space.

Astronauts have always been the public face of the space program. In the 1950s and '60s, it was particularly important to project an image of them as solid, dependable family men. (There wouldn't be a bachelor in space until Jack Swigert flew on Apollo 13 in 1970.)

In the 1950s and '60s, the air force was attempting to perfect rocket aircraft that could break the sound barrier. The men who piloted those experimental aircraft were subjected to extreme environmental stress. It was thought that they might be good candidates for the rigors of space travel.

Naval aviators had to perfect the skills necessary for landing very precisely on a moving aircraft carrier. These were also skills that would be needed for space flight. The stories of these men are told in Tom Wolfe's book and the 1983 motion picture *The Right Stuff*.

Astronaut Jack Swigert was the first unmarried man to reach space as part of the Apollo 13 mission in 1970.

CHAPTER 3

WATCHING THE SKIES

While everyone hopes that missile systems will never have to be used and international conflict will never break out among the stars, the guardians—as members of the USSF are called—are on constant alert. Using the latest technology to scan the skies, they live up to their motto: Semper Supra.

Satellites may be located out in space, but everyone depends on them for many things in their day-to-day lives.

SATELLITES

Satellites are artificial structures that have been launched into orbit around Earth. The first satellite was Sputnik 1, launched by the Soviet Union in 1957. The United States followed with Explorer 1 in 1958. Since then, thousands of satellites have been launched, mainly by the United States and Russia (part of the former Soviet Union). Some satellites are tiny, while others are enormous. For example, the International Space Station, weighing 400 tons (363 metric tons), is considered a satellite.

Currently, satellites are launched into space on rockets. Most U.S. satellite launches are from Vandenberg Space Force Base in California. In the past, satellites have been launched from the space shuttle. The launch window is the precisely timed period when an object can be launched into space and achieve the correct orbit. Satellites have to be placed at exact altitudes in order to complete the tasks for which they are designed. Manned spacecraft need to be launched in such a way that the crew can be safely retrieved if something goes wrong.

All satellites have features in common. The outside of a satellite is called the bus, and it must be sturdy enough to withstand being launched into orbit while protecting its contents. Many satellites run on batteries that store solar power. They also contain a computer that operates the satellite, a radio to transmit data to and from Earth, and an attitude control system (ACS) to steer it in the right direction.

Most satellites are used to collect and transmit data. Some are used for military purposes, such as gathering intelligence, detecting missiles, or relaying encrypted communications. Others are used to gather scientific data. For example, some satellites, like the Hubble Space Telescope, gather data and images from deep space. Other satellites are used to study Earth. For example, NASA has a space flight center that analyzes earth science data collected from satellites.

The Hubble Space Telescope is in orbit around Earth to take pictures of space without interference from Earth's atmosphere. It was launched and has been repaired by astronauts aboard the space shuttle.

Satellites impact everyday lives in many ways. Weather satellites take pictures of weather patterns and storms from orbit. Meteorologists interpret the images and then use other satellites to broadcast routine forecasts and severe weather warnings via television and radio.

Communication satellites use components called transponders. Transponders are a type of radio that receives telephone signals or data on one frequency, then amplifies it and transmits it back to Earth on another frequency.

Weather and communication satellites are typically placed in a geostationary orbit. This means that they stay in the same spot above Earth at an altitude of greater than 22,223 miles (35,764 km) and rotate once every 24 hours with the planet.

Airplanes and ocean vessels depend on data from navigation satellites, which operate in a medium-Earth orbit (MEO) of 1,243 to 22,223 miles (2,000 to 35,764 km) altitude. They also use communication satellites and data from weather satellites. All of this information is critical to keeping supply lines open—and getting goods onto the shelves of stores across the United States and the world.

Phone and email communication, internet commerce, and even the entertainment enjoyed by billions are all conveyed through space and cyberspace. USSF personnel protect both the physical assets that orbit Earth and the computer networks that conduct information.

SPACE OPERATIONS

Satellites form the heart of everything that is done in space. Space operations officers are the ones who work with all those satellites. Some of the things they do may seem obvious—they use satellites to monitor weather, communicate, and gather intelligence. The information they collect is communicated to personnel on the ground and used to deploy troops and equipment.

There are also early warning systems that use radar and computers to scan for incoming missiles. Advance notice of an attack is key to taking appropriate countermeasures, issuing evacuation orders, and summoning emergency aid if needed.

Satellites are also used to track maritime crime. The oceans are so vast that the only way to truly track all activity is from above, via satellite. Crimes committed at sea include pollution, smuggling, poaching, and piracy.

The USSF's 18th Space Control Squadron performs a task that is not obvious when considering space operations. Members use satellites to monitor orbital debris. Of course, these can be natural items, such as meteorites and space dust, but there is a great deal of debris left from human exploration of space. The Department of Defense's Space Surveillance Network (SSN) has cataloged more than 27,000 pieces of orbital debris. This encompasses everything from spacecraft that no longer function to tiny flecks of paint.

Orbital debris moves at very high rates of speed, so even the tiniest fragments can cause damage to vehicles and other satellites. Being aware of what is in orbit and exactly where it is located is a vital task. The area around the International Space Station is closely monitored for debris. If an object large enough to be considered a threat is detected, the station can be moved slightly to avoid impact.

NASA studies have concluded that even if there were no further space launches, the amount of man-made debris currently in orbit is enough to pose a threat to space operations. Finding a safe and effective way to remove the existing debris and reduce the amount of subsequent debris is an ongoing effort. In 2007, a Chinese test to destroy an obsolete satellite with a missile resulted in even more debris.

In addition to the standard requirements for all USSF officers, space operations officers must have a bachelor's or master's degree in a scientific field. Additionally, they need to possess an understanding of space systems and policies and complete Undergraduate Space Training (UST) and additional specialized training.

Space systems operations specialists are enlisted personnel. They operate missile detection systems, aid in satellite launch procedures, and assist in space flight operations. Space systems operations specialists must achieve a minimum Armed Services Vocational Aptitude Battery (ASVAB) score in electronics and complete basic training and other standard requirements.

USSF ENLISTED

Perhaps you're not sure if you want to spend your entire career in the military. Or maybe a college education is proving to be a financial hurdle. Serving as an enlisted airman can be a great way to get valuable technical training that can form the basis for a solid civilian career. Enlisted personnel are also eligible for tuition assistance through the Montgomery G.I. Bill.

USSF enlisted personnel must be between 17 and 39 years of age and have a high school diploma or GED. They need to achieve an ASVAB score of 36 for high school seniors or graduates, or 50 for GED holders. In addition, they must complete 8.5 weeks of Basic Military Training (BMT) and pass a background check. Enlisted airmen are paid from the time they report for BMT. The entry level pay for a basic enlisted airman is $1,785 per month, in addition to housing, food, and medical benefits.

BMT takes place at Joint Base San Antonio Lackland in Texas. Recruits undergo intense physical training in what is generally a very hot climate. They also learn the culture of the military—rising and retiring at specific times, following orders, and maintaining their quarters and belongings to established standards. Recruits are also taught how to wear their uniforms and the proper personal grooming that's expected. A great deal of BMT is designed to make recruits think of themselves as a unit, rather than individuals. Recruits are issued weapons and trained in their roles in the event of a major attack. They're also prepared psychologically for the stress of combat situations.

Specific career paths require a minimum score in certain ASVAB categories. The four categories are mechanical, administrative, electronic, and general. Many USSF careers also require normal color vision. Enlisted airmen generally sign a four-year contract.

One of the most significant problems with orbital debris is that it lingers in the same orbits used by functioning satellites and spacecraft.

USSF OFFICERS

If you think you'd like to make a career in the USSF, becoming an officer might be the right path for you. Officers are more highly paid and learn valuable leadership skills. They're eligible to retire after 20 years of active service. The skills and training acquired as a USSF officer can be parlayed into a successful civilian career. An officer's base pay starts at $3,385.80 per month, in addition to food and housing benefits.

USSF officers must be between the ages of 18 and 39 and graduate from the Air Force Academy (AFA) or complete Officer Training School (OTS) or Air Force Reserve Officer Training Corps (AFROTC).

OTS takes place at Maxwell AFB in Alabama. It includes 30 hours of distance learning and eight weeks of training on the base. The program is designed for college graduates and people with advanced professional training, such as doctors and lawyers. Unlike BMT, which is designed to create units of airmen capable of following orders, OTS exists to train leaders.

Most officers' career paths require at least one college degree and completion of a background security investigation, as well as specialized training. Additionally, normal color vision is a prerequisite for many USSF careers.

CHAPTER 4

PROTECTING THE FLOW OF INFORMATION

War *Games* is a 1983 movie about a teenager who accidentally hacks into the Defense Department's computer system and nearly kicks off a global conflict. While this made a very entertaining premise for a film, the reality is too terrifying to contemplate. The USSF employs cyberspace operations officers and cyber warfare operations officers who protect the sensitive data that moves through cyberspace against hackers and other cybercriminals. They not only defend the United States, they also protect its citizens from cybercrimes, such as identity theft.

MAXWELL AFB

Maxwell Air Force Base, located in Montgomery, Alabama, is home to the Air University. It's where personnel are assigned to complete various forms of specialty training needed for their USSF career path. The university offers many levels of programming, from professional development to granting degrees.

Air University is home to many professional schools, including Officer Training School. The School of Advanced Air and Space Studies is an advanced training program requiring students to write a master-level thesis. The Air Force Institute of Technology is actually five schools, including the Graduate School of Engineering and Management.

Air University is also a center for higher and professional education for enlisted personnel. It includes the Air Force Community College, as well as the Noncommissioned Officer Academy (NCOA) and the Senior Noncommissioned Officer Academy.

The base is located on the site of the Wright brothers' first civilian flight school. It first came into use as an Air Corps base during World War I. The Army Air Corps Tactical School moved to the site in the 1930s, and the Air University was established in 1946. Today it's the site of the Air Education and Training Command, as well as the Junior ROTC Flight Academy.

CYBERSPACE

The word "cyberspace" was coined by science fiction writer William Gibson in 1982. Today, it is used to refer to the virtual places of the internet—the digital world that exists due to the connection of computer networks all around the planet. The pages and places available online are considered to exist in cyberspace.

The USSF helps to protect the information—civilian and military—that moves through cyberspace from hackers.

Although cyberspace is not a physical place, a great deal of valuable information exists there. Criminals can cause enormous damage if data is not protected. That is why providing cyberspace security is one of the USSF's main objectives.

CYBERSPACE SECURITY

Today, the information that powers our increasingly global society moves through cyberspace. The internet has brought a new level of convenience to our day-to-day lives. It is possible to order and pay for almost any sort of product and have it delivered in just a few days. People can purchase movies or other content without moving from the living room sofa. Dinner can be ordered and delivered within an hour. People pay bills online and transfer money from one bank account to another.

Most of these tasks can be accomplished from the latest smartphone models. Unfortunately, however, the same technology that makes human lives so much easier can also provide opportunities for criminals. Hackers are criminals who steal private information from the internet. They might use programs known as viruses or malware to make computers malfunction. Sometimes, they trick people into entering sensitive information on a fraudulent website. Then, they use the stolen information to cause malicious mischief or steal money—or even more sensitive information.

Social media accounts can be vulnerable if they use a weak password. It can be easy to accidentally click on a sketchy pop-up ad that downloads a computer virus. These are examples of the work of hackers and other cybercriminals. Some of the things they do are just a nuisance. It is fairly easy to straighten out a social media account by communicating directly with the company and answering security questions. Viruses can often be fixed with commercial software programs that are easy to obtain.

However, cybercriminals can be more dangerous. Two major problems in the modern world are credit card fraud and identity theft. These are more severe crimes. They can cost people a lot of money and damage their credit rating. Correcting this sort of crime might require filing a police report, opening a new bank account, or even dealing with the Internal Revenue Service (IRS). This can waste a lot of time and be costly.

At an even higher level is the sort of information in banks' computer systems—thousands of people's bank account numbers, credit card numbers, and sensitive personal information, plus all the systems banks use to communicate with other banks. Retail stores and hotel chains also have enormous amounts of financial information in their computer systems. When a large company discovers that information has been stolen from their system, they make a public announcement. This can damage their reputation and cause them to lose customers, in addition to the cost of finding and repairing the breach in their system.

This is all pretty serious stuff—and that is only considering the threats to civilian computer systems. The kind of information carried on military computer networks includes launch codes for missiles, command and control information for satellites and spacecraft, and orders for troop movements. Protecting cyberspace is a vital task.

Cyber warfare operations officers are in charge of cyberspace weapons systems. They ensure the security of military operations in cyberspace and prevent unseen attacks on computer networks from having real-world consequences.

Most USSF personnel work remotely, but the information they provide is vital to troops on the front lines.

Cyberspace operations officers analyze and assess the information provided by various computer networks. They are experts in intelligence gathering and communication systems. They collate intelligence information, weather data, and other resources to provide risk assessment for planning operations.

Cyber warfare operations officers and cyberspace operations officers need to have a bachelor's degree in a STEM field, plus a strong working knowledge of information technology (IT), electronics theory, telecommunications, and cryptography. In addition, they need to complete the undergraduate cyberspace training and additional mission qualification training at Maxwell Air Force Base in Alabama.

Cyber surety specialists are enlisted personnel who are responsible for protecting computer networks from cyberattacks. It is their job to assess systems for possible vulnerabilities that criminals could exploit and fix those weaknesses before an attack can occur. They ensure that the networks that manage lines of communication and information are secured to the highest government standards. To qualify, potential candidates must achieve a minimum score in the general ASVAB category and complete additional technical training. They must possess a working knowledge of information systems.

According to the Bureau of Labor Statistics, cyberspace security is a fast-growing field. After leaving the USSF, trained professionals can expect to earn highly competitive salaries in civilian careers.

What is now known as the internet began in the 1960s as a project in the U.S. Department of Defense. Internet access became popular in the 1990s, and it is now a global phenomenon.

THE SPACE SHUTTLE

The space shuttle was the world's first reusable spacecraft. Since the 1950s, various aerospace organizations have been trying to design a reusable "space plane." The prototype shuttle was named the *Enterprise*, following intervention from the cast and fans of the original *Star Trek* TV show. This helped attract popular support for the project.

The first shuttle to fly in space was *Columbia*. It launched from Kennedy Space Center on April 12, 1981, the 20th anniversary of Yuri Gagarin's first space flight. It returned safely to Earth two days later. Sally Ride (1951–2012) became the first American woman to fly in space aboard the shuttle *Challenger* in 1983. The shuttle program would continue for 135 missions, ending when *Atlantis* landed safely on July 21, 2011.

During its 20 years, the program lost two shuttles to catastrophic accidents, *Challenger* in 1986 and *Columbia* in 2003. In total, 14 astronauts were lost. Their memories are honored with memorials at Arlington National Cemetery.

The shuttle was launched into space like a rocket and returned to land like a plane instead of splashing down into the ocean. It contained a payload bay that was used to carry things like satellites into orbit and a robotic arm that could be used for repairs. The space shuttle was used to build the International Space Station and launch and repair the Hubble Space Telescope.

Currently, SpaceX is conducting launches with reused boosters and capsules. With diligent research and cooperation between relevant agencies, the "space plane" might become a reality.

The historic launch of *Columbia* changed the field of space flight forever as the first "space shuttle" to successfully launch.

CHAPTER 5

CREATING NEW TECHNOLOGY

In 1941, when Jim Crow laws were widespread in the South, President Franklin D. Roosevelt signed Executive Order 8802, the Prohibition of Discrimination in the Defense Industry. That legislation enabled Dorothy Vaughan to be hired by the Langley Memorial Aeronautical Laboratory in 1943. Although Virginia was still a segregated state, this executive order was the beginning of the realization that space exploration would require the finest minds on the planet—and that prejudice could have no place in the equation.

The U.S. Astronaut Hall of Fame at Kennedy Space Center is a great place to learn about the men and women who have made the idea of a career in space a reality.

A PLACE FOR HISTORIC FIRSTS

By the time NACA transitioned into NASA in 1958, there were no longer segregated work groups, lunchrooms, or restrooms. The first Black American selected for the space program was air force astronaut Robert H. Lawrence in 1967. He perished in an aircraft accident before he could fly in space.

In 1978, NASA selected a pool of astronaut candidates to train for the first space shuttle missions.

The group included women and people of color for the first time. In 1983, the first American woman and the first Black American would fly in space, followed in 1985 by the first Asian American.

NASA astronauts are extraordinarily accomplished individuals. While a college degree was a prerequisite for the Mercury 7, many of today's astronauts hold multiple degrees. For example, Dr. Mae Jemison—the first Black American woman to fly in space—is a physician and engineer who speaks multiple languages.

MARY JACKSON

Mary Jackson (1921–2005) was one of the subjects of the book and movie *Hidden Figures*. She was the first female African American engineer at NASA. Due to segregation and prevailing employment policies, it's possible she was the only female African American aeronautical engineer at the time.

She was part of the segregated West Area Computing Group, where the advanced mathematics necessary to compute space flight trajectories were calculated by hand. Engineer Kazimierz Czarnecki offered her a position on one of his projects and encouraged her to become qualified as an engineer. To do so, she needed to take graduate courses offered only at a segregated high school. She required special permission from the City of Hampton to attend the school. In 1958, she was promoted to the position of engineer.

In 2019, Mary Jackson, along with Katherine Johnson, Dorothy Vaughan, and Christine Darden, was posthumously awarded the Congressional Gold Medal. In June 2020, NASA named a building in her honor.

Jackson, shown here, worked as an engineer for NASA for nearly three decades. In 1979, she became the manager of Langley's Federal Women's Program, where she worked hard to hire and promote female engineers and mathematicians for NASA.

DEVELOPMENTAL ENGINEERS

At every phase of space exploration, scientists have determined what was needed to achieve an objective, and engineers have stepped up and made their vision a reality. Less than a century ago, spaceflight was pure fantasy. Every single piece of equipment had to be imagined, designed, and built to withstand the rigors of space.

Aerospace engineers have had to figure out lots of big jobs:

- How to launch objects into—and then beyond—Earth's atmosphere
- How to build objects that will function in extreme cold and zero gravity
- How to build objects that can be launched into space and then retrieved intact
- How to build spacecraft that can support human life in a totally hostile environment

These are pretty impressive achievements—especially when considering that the Wright brothers' first flight was in 1903, and the first manned space flight was in 1961. In a span of less than 60 years, technology and scientific understanding took humanity beyond the planet.

The first objects launched over long distances were rockets. They were weapons designed to explode and cause damage. A manned spacecraft needed to remain intact and functioning and preserve human life. Human beings are only able to fully function

The USSF employs developmental engineers whose job it is to solve problems and build things.

on the surface of Earth. People need a breathable atmosphere, and human bodies function best within a specific range of gravity and pressure. None of that exists in space. Engineers have had to work with medical doctors to figure out how to keep people alive in space. There are many details to consider. Of course, astronauts need oxygen to breathe, but what about the carbon dioxide and other waste products they exhale? How can waste products be removed from a sealed environment?

Alan Shepard was the first American in space. His launch was delayed for several hours, and he needed to use the restroom. Unfortunately, he was strapped into his capsule and could not move. Unsealing it to let him out would have meant scrubbing, or canceling, the mission. NASA scientists did not know what would happen if fluid was released inside the sealed, pressurized spacesuit.

No one thought he would be in the flight suit for so long. Ultimately, he was instructed to "do it in the suit," which shorted out some sensors. Needless to say, NASA put people to work on that particular problem. The device made for John Glenn's later flight is in the collection of the Smithsonian National Air and Space Museum. Engineers create the equipment that makes space travel a reality.

Sometimes, they have to find solutions very quickly. In the movie *Apollo 13*, there a scene in which a group of NASA engineers are handed a box of odd parts and told that they needed to adapt a

The new technology being designed and built by engineers requires software and computer programs to make it all work.

square filter to fit into a round hole. That is the sort of problem developmental engineers face in their work.

In the early days of the space program, multiple agencies were trying to find solutions for problems independently. Today, the USSF is partnering with other American and allied agencies in cooperative discovery. For example, a 2021 NASA project to alter the path of an asteroid was launched from Vandenberg Space Force Base aboard a SpaceX vessel. Part of the project also entailed launching an Italian satellite.

Developmental engineers are highly qualified personnel. They are required to have at least a bachelor's degree in engineering, plus 12 months of experience. A master's degree or Ph.D. can substitute for some of that required work experience. In addition, they must complete Defense Acquisition University, the Air Force Flight Test Engineer Course, and a course in Acquisition Fundamentals or Fundamentals of System Acquisition Management.

After a career in the USSF, an aerospace engineer can look forward to a highly rewarding civilian career. According to the Bureau of Labor Statistics, the field is growing, with an average annual salary of well over $100,000.

COMPUTER SYSTEMS PROGRAMMING

Computer systems programming specialists are USSF enlisted personnel who create the software and computer programs needed for space operations.

Besides the usual requirements for enlisted personnel, computer systems programming specialists must achieve a minimum score in the general category of the ASVAB. Then they need to complete 70 days of technical training at Keesler Air Force Base. Finally, they are required to complete the Computer Systems Programming Initial Skills course and achieve a minimum score of 71 on the Air Force Electronic Data Processing Test.

Computer science is a major field both inside and outside of the military. After leaving the service, a computer programmer or software developer can expect to find a solid job with great earning potential in the civilian world.

DOROTHY VAUGHAN

Dorothy Vaughan (1910–2008) was a contemporary of Mary Jackson's and Katherine Johnson's. She's remembered as the first African American manager at NASA.

She was hired by NACA, the predecessor of NASA, in 1943 as an expert mathematician, or "computer." Her initial employment was made possible because of an executive order by President Roosevelt prohibiting discrimination in defense industries. She was appointed head of the West Area Computing Group in 1949, when Jim Crow laws were still in full force in Virginia.

In 1958, she and many of her colleagues moved to NASA's Analysis and Computation Division (ACD), working with the new electronic IBM mainframe computers. The new agency was no longer segregated by race or gender. She became an expert in FORTRAN, a computer programming language first used in 1954.

CHAPTER 6

THE PEOPLE BEHIND THE SCENES

The USSF is technically part of the U.S. Air Force, similar to how the Marine Corps is part of the U.S. Navy. Because of this, some of the traditional military support career paths, such as medicine, law, and religion, fall under the umbrella of the air force. The USSF does not have its own medical, legal, or chaplain contingent.

Although jobs working with missile and satellite technology are the obvious career choices in the USSF, some traditional military career paths exist in a modified form for those who want to serve in this branch.

ASVAB

The Armed Services Vocational Aptitude Battery (ASVAB) is a set of 10 timed tests used to determine eligibility to enlist in the armed forces. Unlike the ACT or SAT, which are designed to predict success in college, the ASVAB is designed to predict success as an enlisted person in the armed forces.

The results of four of the tests (word knowledge, paragraph comprehension, arithmetic reasoning, and mathematics knowledge) are combined into one score called the Armed Forces Qualification Test (AFQT). This is used to determine if you're eligible to enlist.

The remaining tests are used to find the best job placement for you within the service. The categories are general science, electronics information, auto information, shop information, mechanical comprehension, and assembling objects. Some USSF career paths require minimum scores in one or more of these tests.

The test is given only in English. This is because orders are issued in English and recruits must be able to follow orders instantly with no communication errors.

At an initial interview, a recruiter will determine if you seem like a good candidate for enlistment. If they think you might make a good recruit, they'll schedule you to take the ASVAB.

ACQUISITION MANAGER

Acquisition managers are responsible for obtaining the correct supplies for USSF units. It is their job to oversee the order and delivery of critical parts and supplies. Since the USSF works in space, this can include finding a special vendor who manufactures what is needed, or even coordinating with engineers to create specific items. It also involves having materials transported to the correct locations.

The Space and Missile Systems Center is responsible for acquiring and developing the materials the USSF uses. This includes equipment for space launches, GPS, communications, range systems, and control systems for space vehicles. Items required for working in space often need to be designed and built to accommodate the specific requirements of a project. This might require many levels of design and experimentation.

Acquisition managers are responsible for finding all the "right stuff" for the USSF—and then making sure that it is delivered wherever it needs to be!

Many questions need to be asked and answered when designing an object for use in space:

- What function does this object need to perform?
- What physical conditions will it have to perform under?
- Will it be automatic or controlled from Earth?
- How will this item be launched into space?
- How will it be repaired if necessary?
- Will it transmit data, or will it need to be retrieved intact?
- Does this object need to support human life?

It might take input from engineers, technicians, and computer programmers to complete a design for a new piece of space equipment. If it is intended to be an object that people will inhabit, feedback from medical doctors or psychiatrists might be needed as well.

For example, how do astronauts write in space? Regular pens require gravity for the ink to flow, so they would not work. Pencils posed the hazard of bits of lead breaking off and becoming lodged in delicate electronics. NASA required a pen to write in zero gravity, in extremes of heat or cold, in any position, and not leak.

The Fisher Pen Company designed a pen with a pressurized ink cartridge that fulfilled NASA's requirements. Contrary to popular myth, the project was not funded by tax dollars, and Soviet cosmonauts used them too. Like other technology that was developed for space but found a market on Earth, the Fisher Space Pens are sold to regular civilians. They are still used by NASA and can be found aboard the International Space Station.

NASA has a longstanding practice of commissioning items from civilian companies. Many of those items have gone on to become common consumer goods. These include:

- Black & Decker's DustBuster, which uses technology invented for working on the moon.
- Foster Grant's scratch-resistant lenses, derived from technology used to create astronaut helmets.
- Goodyear radial tires are made of a material invented for the Viking Lander.
- Honeywell's smoke detectors with adjustable sensitivity.
- The technology used to create camera phones.

Air purification, water filtration, CAT scans, MRIs, and infrared thermometers were all invented for the space program. Ice-resistant planes and grooved pavement were developed for the space shuttle and are now used at commercial airports. Space technology is also responsible for driving the innovations supporting the portable computer and the computer mouse.

Without question, today's USSF acquisition manager is far from the traditional quartermaster found in other service branches. In addition to the standard requirements for officers, acquisition managers need to have a bachelor's degree and knowledge of the system they will be working with. They also have to complete Air Force Acquisition qualifying courses.

INTELLIGENCE OFFICERS

A great deal of military intelligence is gathered through the use of keyhole satellites. These are structures similar to the Hubble Telescope, but instead of being focused out into deep space, they are focused on Earth. This type of satellite has been used for more than 30 years.

Intelligence officers analyze data gathered from satellites and use it to help troops on the ground. They can identify enemy troops, weapons, or even dangerous weather conditions.

Keyhole satellites take digital photographs from an altitude of about 200 miles (322 km). They can see objects at ground level that are larger than 5 inches (12.7 cm). Vandenberg Space Force Base in California is the primary launch site for American satellites.

Because the satellites are moving through space, they do not remain still long enough to take video, but a trained analyst can study the images to detect

AIR FORCE RESERVE

The Air Force Reserves are part-time or standby units that may be called into active duty in an emergency situation. Applicants with no prior military service must be between the ages of 18 and 39, be U.S. citizens or permanent residents, and have a high school diploma or GED.

Reservists are required to complete the same 8.5-week BMT as other enlisted personnel at Lackland AFB in San Antonio, Texas. After graduation and additional technical training, reservists can expect to serve one weekend a month and an additional two weeks a year. Reservists have many training and educational opportunities and receive a benefits package.

The Reserves can be a good place to get training and educational benefits at the start of your career. Airmen and women nearing the end of their military career sometimes use a stint in the Reserves to complete their enlistment or academy commitment or to transition back to civilian life.

At this time, a Space Force Reserve is in the planning stages.

troop movement or the placement of equipment. Intelligence officers obtain and analyze the data used to plan missions. In addition to the usual prerequisites for officers, they need to have a bachelor's degree in either science, humanities, social sciences, structured analysis, engineering, or mathematics. Experience in a foreign language is a plus. After completing the Intelligence Officer Initial Skills course, they must also complete required training courses and 12 months of commissioned service performing intelligence functions.

CIVILIAN CAREERS

Military bases are supported by civilians from a large number of career fields. Some of them are civilian experts assigned to military projects. Others work in support functions—everything from secretarial jobs to teaching at base schools to providing care for working animals on the base. The air force is an equal opportunity employer with regard to civilians. There is no discrimination based on race, gender, ethnic background, religion, disability, or pregnancy status. Spouses of active-duty personnel are given preference for civilian jobs at the base where they are stationed.

Military bases are often major employers in their area. Vandenberg Space Force Base supports a population of 15,000.

OPTIONS FOR ENLISTED PERSONNEL

Cyber systems operations specialists design, install, and maintain the servers and systems used by the USSF. They are also the ones who repair systems when something goes wrong. In addition to the standard requirements for enlisted personnel, they must achieve the required minimum score in the ASVAB general category, and they are required to complete the Cyber Systems Operations Initial Skills course at Keesler AFB in Mississippi.

Cyber transport systems specialists maintain the communications infrastructure and equipment. This position requires a valid driver's license, a minimum score in the electronics category of the ASVAB, and a solid understanding of network principles, as well as more than four months of technical training at Keesler AFB.

Cable and antenna systems specialists install and maintain cable and wireless systems. Therefore, they need to be in good physical condition and able to tolerate both enclosed spaces and heights. In addition, they are required to have a valid driver's license, achieve a minimum score in both the mechanical and electronic categories of the ASVAB, and complete 80 days of technical training at Sheppard AFB in Texas.

Obviously, all these skills are in demand in the civilian job market, so enlisted members of the USSF in these careers can look forward to a solid job outlook when they leave the armed forces. There are plenty of options for civilian telecommunications equipment installers and computer support specialists, both positions that have strong civilian pay ranges.

CHAPTER 7

GETTING THERE

The U.S. Space Force is all about technology—using it, troubleshooting and repairing it, and even developing it. Therefore, for anyone who wants a career in the USSF, it makes sense to earn at least a bachelor's degree in a STEM field. Of course, a master's or Ph.D. will open up even more exciting prospects.

As of 2021, the USSF does not have its own service academy. The best path available to most recruits is through the Air Force Academy (AFA) or by earning a degree in a STEM field at a civilian college or university.

THE AIR FORCE ACADEMY

Attending the AFA requires a nomination by the vice president of the United States or a member of Congress and a commitment to serve in the air force or space force as a commissioned officer after graduation. The length of service will vary by the career path and degree selected by the recruit. Most graduates sign on as part of an eight-year commitment. Five years must be served as active duty, and the remaining three may be served as a reservist. Graduates who have completed pilot training have a 10-year commitment.

The Air Force Academy is located in Colorado Springs. It was founded in 1954. The first female cadets were admitted in 1976.

The AFA has offered a space curriculum since 1965. It was one of the first accredited undergraduate programs of its kind. The first AFA graduate to fly in space was Karol Bobko, who piloted the space shuttle *Challenger* in 1983. More than three dozen AFA graduates have gone on to become NASA astronauts.

Attending the AFA is free of charge for qualified recruits, meaning that recruits do not have to carry student debt after graduation. The AFA is regarded as one of the top universities in the United States. An outstanding education coupled with practical experience make graduates top candidates for any civilian career after serving the necessary commitment.

In contrast, earning a four-year STEM degree from a civilian school can cost $100,000—or even more—in tuition and other fees. However, there are ways to reduce the financial burden, such as taking core credits at a community college and then transferring to a different institution. In addition, many state universities offer a fine education for far less cost than attending an Ivy League school. Many resources offer grants or scholarships instead of student loans, but these can be competitive.

The Reserve Officers' Training Corps (ROTC) is another path to a career as an air force officer. The program offers financial aid and practical leadership training. ROTC cadets are full-time college students. They are required to take special classes and officer training programs. They must maintain a 2.0 grade point average—or 2.5 for scholarship cadets. In addition, cadets must take the Air Force

Air Force ROTC is offered at more than 1,100 colleges and universities across the United States. Scholarship cadets graduate from the program with marketable skills, a paying job, and no student debt.

Officer Qualification Test, which evaluates various aptitudes to determine their best career path.

Scholarship cadets must meet air force physical fitness standards in order to retain their financial assistance. Non-scholarship cadets must work toward those standards if they wish to be commissioned. There are additional physical requirements for those who wish to take flight training. Air Force ROTC cadets can be assigned to the USSF upon graduation.

ROTC programs are open to high school students, college students, and enlisted airmen. After graduation, cadets are commissioned as second lieutenants and complete the required service commitment—4 years for many career paths and 10 years for pilots.

The Reserves and National Guard offer opportunities for technical training and financial aid for a recruit's education while they serve part time. Requirements for people without prior military experience are similar to the requirements for active duty enlisted personnel. Although there are not yet Space Force National Guard units, there are National Guard personnel engaged in space operations.

PREPARING FOR WORK IN SPACE

For anyone whose dream is to fly in space, the USSF is the best option. To qualify as a NASA astronaut, candidates must have a master's degree in a STEM field, have earned two years of related experience,

AIR NATIONAL GUARD

Like the Air Force Reserve, the Air National Guard (ANG) is a way to serve part-time—one weekend a month and an additional two weeks a year. Guard members are generally stationed locally. In addition to being standby units for active federal military duty, Guard units are also the purview of the governor of the state where they're located. For example, the governor can call up Guard units to help with large-scale accidents or natural disasters in an emergency.

Guard members must attend BMT at Lackland AFB as well as technical school. They receive many of the same benefits as other airmen, including the use of base facilities, travel privileges (depending on space availability), and access to VA programs. The ANG provides career training and educational benefits, but it also recruits professionals, particularly in medical fields.

At this time, there isn't a plan for forming National Guard units of the USSF, but that might change in the future.

and be able to pass the astronaut physical. Alternatively, astronaut candidates can be doctoral candidates in a STEM field, medical doctors, or test pilot school graduates. A stint in the USSF can help with all of these goals.

Young people, for whom college and a career are still years away, are able to prepare for an eventual shot at the USSF. Any military career requires good grades and good physical conditioning. Practical skills like first aid and swimming are also helpful. Since career paths in the USSF require advanced computer skills, taking any classes available will provide an advantage. Science fairs and Maker Faires are also great activities.

Team sports and group activities such as band are great for learning to work well with others. These activities also look good on applications for both college and the military. In addition, organizations that promote service and good citizenship—such as scouting and 4-H—are also great experience.

Martial arts require practice and discipline to move up through the ranks. This is good practice for life in the military—and also helps keep people physically fit.

Activities such as scouts or martial arts, which require members to achieve different ranks, are great experience for the military. In particular, achieving the rank of Eagle Scout is highly regarded as a demonstration of outstanding leadership skills.

As a branch of the armed forces, the USSF is an equal opportunity employer. However, recruits must meet the physical requirements of their job descriptions and may be disqualified from consideration due to past criminal history or drug use. To qualify for enlistment, recruits must be able to pass the ASVAB in English. The test is given only in English because orders are given in English. Airmen must be able to understand orders with no language barrier or confusion.

THE AIR FORCE WORLD CLASS ATHLETE PROGRAM

Did you know that the first active-duty U.S. military member to win an Olympic gold medal was an airman? Malvin G. Whitfield was one of the Tuskegee Airmen. He won gold medals in track and field events at the 1948 and 1952 Olympics. He trained by running on airfields between missions.

The Air Force World Class Athlete Program (WCAP) began in the 1990s to honor his legacy. The program allows active-duty airmen to train for world and Olympic competition. WCAP participants must maintain the standards of their chosen career path while training. In addition, they often participate in public relations activities.

CHAPTER 8

LIFE ON EARTH

Joining the USSF or any other branch of the military is a huge decision. After all, the armed forces exist first and foremost to defend the United States. By putting on the uniform, all soldiers are deliberately choosing to place themselves in harm's way. Active-duty members can be deployed anywhere in the world. They may have to leave their families for long periods of time. They could be injured or even lose their lives. Veterans of combat situations often suffer long-term mental effects. All of these factors can stress a marriage to the point of separation or divorce.

The government recognizes the stress and hardship involved in military service and provides ample compensation and benefits. Enlisted airmen and women receive a regular amount of base pay depending on their rank. Officers are generally paid more, and again the amount varies based on rank. Besides a competitive base salary, airmen and guardians have access to complete medical and life insurance packages and other benefits.

LIVING ON A BASE

Air force and space force bases are complete, enclosed communities. The day begins with reveille in the morning and ends with taps in the evening. Food, housing, and medical and dental care are provided for military personnel. Unmarried airmen and women live in dormitories, similar to college dorms. These dorms have laundry facilities, recreation rooms, and community kitchens. There is a tax-free commissary, or grocery store, available. Bases also include a fitness center, pharmacy, and medical and dental facilities.

A typical base will also include a chapel, bank, car repair facility, and emergency services. The base exchange (BX) is where personnel can purchase just about anything for lower prices than at a civilian superstore. Some bases also feature education centers and libraries available to personnel to continue their education or earn a degree.

For married personnel, there are sections of the base devoted to family-style housing. When they have the option to live off base, a housing allowance is provided. Many bases have elementary schools, after-school programs, and child care facilities. Playgrounds and youth sports teams are also available. Medical care is free for the families of military personnel, and dental care is discounted.

Exercise and recreation are valuable tools for mental and physical health. Chaplains and counselors are available for military personnel and their families. Many bases have pools, parks, and other sports facilities. Bases in some locations might even have stables or a golf course.

Military bases employ civilians in many professional fields, ranging from animal care to accounting to medical specialties. Qualified spouses of active-duty service people receive preferential placement.

All airmen and women receive 30 days of paid vacation per year. In addition, they can use air force transportation on a space-available basis and stay at an inn on base for less than a stay at a civilian hotel.

WHERE ON EARTH?

The USSF's bases are located in the continental United States, clustered in California, Colorado, and Florida.

The United States has been launching rockets from Florida since 1950. Before that, the first few experimental rocket launches took place in White Sands, New Mexico, where test projects could crash into the barren desert. As rockets became larger and more powerful, launches were moved to the coast so that rockets could fly over the open ocean and crash there if necessary. Additionally, Florida is close to the equator. By launching to the east from Florida, the rocket's momentum is aided by Earth's natural rotation. This means that less fuel is needed to launch. It also means that larger rockets with larger payloads can be launched.

The USSF has most of its bases in California, Colorado, and Florida.

Commercial space companies SpaceX and Blue Origin also have facilities in Florida. SpaceX has a platform where rocket stages can be recovered after delivering their payload. The European Space Agency (ESA) launches from French Guiana for similar reasons.

Rockets are also launched from Vandenberg Space Force Base in California. Vandenberg's location near Lompoc, California, allows the USSF to launch rockets to the south without endangering local populations. This allows the rockets to achieve trajectories for a polar orbit. This type of orbit is impossible to achieve from a Florida launch without flying over major population centers.

Minuteman Missile National Historic Site in South Dakota is a remnant of the Cold War. Thousands of missiles were held in readiness against the possibility of a Soviet attack under the watchful eyes of air force personnel.

Some air force bases dedicated to missile defense in the Colorado area are being designated as Space Force bases. During the Cold War, missile sites were constructed in the Midwest. This was because the sites were farther from the coast, giving them more time to react to a launch from a submarine. It is also a good vantage point to launch missiles toward Russia. The trajectory would take them through Canadian airspace and across the pole. The Great Plains are also less densely populated than the coasts in the event of an accident or attack.

BENEFITS FOR THE REST OF YOUR LIFE

The U.S. Air Force and Space Force offer several programs for continuing education. These can range from specialty programs offered at military facilities to partial or even full tuition at a civilian college. For outstanding athletes eligible for international or Olympic-level competition, there is the potential to qualify for the Air Force World Class Athlete Program.

For those who choose a career in the military, there is a full retirement package. Airmen and women are eligible to retire after 20 years of service. The U.S. Department of Veterans Affairs (VA) has many programs to help veterans transition back to civilian life. For example, it can help with medical and mental health issues resulting from combat. It also has programs for continuing education and assisting veterans who want to go into business for themselves.

After leaving the USSF, civilian career prospects are very good. Jobs involving computers and technology are always in demand. According to the Bureau of Labor Statistics, computer systems analysts and information systems managers can expect to earn excellent salaries in civilian fields.

Northrop Grumman participates in the Department of Defense's Skillbridge Military Internship Program. This is a program to help veterans transition into the civilian workforce. The USSF training and skillset is a good match for an aerospace company.

THE U.S. DEPARTMENT OF VETERANS AFFAIRS

The U.S. Department of Veterans Affairs (VA) exists to help veterans with all aspects of their post-military life. It has programs to help veterans transition back to civilian life, including employment and education programs, and home loans and insurance.

The VA provides medical care and mental health programs for veterans who've been injured or disabled in combat. It also aids veterans who've had trouble returning to civilian life with issues such as substance abuse or homelessness. The VA Health Administration is the largest integrated health care system in the U.S. Each veteran's benefit package is tailored to them, taking into account their length of service and whether an injury or condition is a direct result of their military activity.

The VA also administers the National Cemetery System, ensuring a dignified resting place for those who have served their country.

EQUAL OPPORTUNITIES

While other branches of the military are mostly male, the highly technical USSF is proving surprisingly equitable to female personnel. As of 2020, 22 percent of officers and 21 percent of enlisted personnel in the Department of the Air Force, which oversees the USSF, were women, as well as almost 30 percent of its civilian staff. The USSF boasts a female three star general in its command staff and female chief master sergeants.

EXECUTIVE ORDER

ESTABLISHING THE PRESIDENT'S COMMITTEE ON
EQUALITY OF TREATMENT AND OPPORTUNITY IN
THE ARMED SERVICES

WHEREAS it is essential that there be maintained in the armed services of the United States the highest standards of democracy, with equality of treatment and opportunity for all those who serve in our country's defense:

NOW, THEREFORE, by virtue of the authority vested in me as President of the United States, by the Constitution and the statutes of the United States, and as Commander in Chief of the armed services, it is hereby ordered as follows:

1. It is hereby declared to be the policy of the President that there shall be equality of treatment and opportunity for all persons in the armed services without regard to race, color, religion or national origin. This policy shall be put into effect as rapidly as possible, having due regard to the time required to effectuate any necessary changes without impairing efficiency or morale.

2. There shall be created in the National Military Establishment an advisory committee to be known as the President's Committee on Equality of Treatment and Opportunity in the Armed Services, which shall be composed of seven members to be designated by the President.

3. The Committee is authorized on behalf of the President to examine into the rules, procedures and practices of the armed services in order to determine in what respect such rules, procedures and practices may be altered or improved with a view to carrying out the policy of this order. The Committee shall confer and advise with the Secretary of Defense, the Secretary

- 2 -

of the Army, the Secretary of the Navy, and the Secretary of the Air Force, and shall make such recommendations to the President and to said Secretaries as in the judgment of the Committee will effectuate the policy hereof.

4. All executive departments and agencies of the Federal Government are authorized and directed to cooperate with the Committee in its work, and to furnish the Committee such information or the services of such persons as the Committee may require in the performance of its duties.

5. When requested by the Committee to do so, persons in the armed services or in any of the executive departments and agencies of the Federal Government shall testify before the Committee and shall make available for the use of the Committee such documents and other information as the Committee may require.

6. The Committee shall continue to exist until such time as the President shall terminate its existence by Executive order.

Harry Truman

THE WHITE HOUSE,
July 26, 1948.

9981

The U.S. armed forces were officially desegregated in 1948 when President Truman signed Executive Order 9981.

Most space force assignments are remote, meaning that personnel are operating systems in space from bases clustered in California, Colorado, and Florida. This reduces the possibility of moving every few years, an issue associated with other branches of the armed services. There are also currently no "front line" assignments. These factors can be attractive to people who wish to have families.

ASTRONAUTS AT ARLINGTON NATIONAL CEMETERY

Flying at supersonic speeds and leaving Earth's atmosphere are dangerous endeavors. Many pilots have given their lives in the quest to go higher, further, and faster. Since test pilots and early astronauts were often military personnel, they were eligible to be interred at Arlington National Cemetery. Astronauts from the Mercury, Gemini, Apollo, and space shuttle programs are buried there.

Gus Grissom (1926–1967) was a distinguished air force fighter pilot and the second American in space. As the pilot of Gemini 3, he became the first American to fly in space more than once. He and Roger Chaffee (1935–1967) both died in the Apollo I launch pad fire and are buried in separate graves in Section 3.

The crews of the space shuttles *Challenger* and *Columbia* are also honored on America's most sacred ground. The commingled remains of the crews are buried beneath their respective monuments in Section 46. Five of the fourteen astronauts whose remains could be identified also have separate graves.

Brave astronauts who lost their lives in support of the U.S. space program are buried at Arlington National Cemetery.

The ethnic and racial mix of the air force is not quite as equal, however. As of 2021, the composition of the air force was 71 percent white, 15 percent African American, and about 16 percent Hispanic or Latino, with many officers being white. Steps are being taken to address this disparity.

FAMOUS FIRSTS

1941	Prohibition of discrimination in the defense industry
1947	U.S. Air Force established
1948	Desegregation of the armed forces
1948	Esther McGowin Blake becomes the first woman to enlist in the air force
1954	Air Force Academy established
1967	Women are allowed to be promoted to the rank of general
1970	Women are allowed to command units that include men
1976	First female cadets at American service academies
2019	U.S. Space Force established

CHAPTER 9

THE FUTURE ISN'T FAR

Less than a century ago, the idea of space flight was a fantasy. Now, humanity occupies a world in which people live and work on space stations. Private companies—not just governments—can launch spacecraft. Celebrity tourists, as well as scientists, have flown in space. There are many new job opportunities and technology to explore. The Bureau of Labor Statistics does not track data related explicitly to space industries, but it projects substantial growth in career paths such as engineering and science, which are involved in working in space. Any education and experience in science or engineering can easily be applied to the civilian job market. This is an excellent time to consider a career in space.

SpaceX is a private aerospace corporation owned by Elon Musk. One of its goals is to create reusable spacecraft to reduce waste and be more cost-effective.

JOHN GLENN

Senator John Glenn (1921–2016) was a Marine Corps fighter pilot who served with distinction in World War II and the Korean War. He flew 59 combat missions in WWII and a total of 90 in Korea.

Following the Korean War, he became a naval test pilot. In 1957, he set a transcontinental speed record, flying from Los Angeles to New York. He was one of the Mercury 7 astronauts and, in 1962, became the first American to orbit Earth.

He wanted to be part of the moon landing program, but it's believed he was considered too valuable a public relations asset to risk in further space flight in the early days of NASA.

He was elected to the Senate for the state of Ohio in 1974 and served four consecutive terms by popular vote. In 1998, at the age of 77, he became the oldest human to fly in space. He participated in a nine-day mission aboard the space shuttle *Discovery*, in part to study the effects of space travel on the aging process.

His achievements—both military and civilian—were honored with many medals and citations. These included the NASA Distinguished Service Medal and the Congressional Space Medal of Honor. Perhaps the most memorable were not one, but two, ticker tape parades in New York City. The first was after his historic flight in 1962 and the second when he returned from his shuttle mission in 1998.

Senator Glenn is buried at Arlington National Cemetery.

John Glenn's *Friendship 7* capsule is on display at the Smithsonian's National Air and Space Museum. The museum is a great place to see America's milestones in space exploration.

STEM EDUCATION

The education necessary to succeed in high-tech jobs can prove a significant financial stumbling block. A career in space requires at least one college degree in a STEM field. Of course, those who pursue their education further are often the first in line for high-paying and highly competitive careers. The USSF is the right place to start a career for many young people. The military provides a variety of opportunities to achieve academic excellence without incurring student debt. In addition to programs that aid with tuition costs, the USSF provides specialist training programs. Those who are selected for these programs get to work with cutting-edge technology. They also learn leadership and teamwork skills, which are valuable in any professional setting.

Students in high school who think that a career in the USSF is the right path for them can talk to their family and guidance counselor for advice. Entrance to the AFA is very competitive and involves many steps, so it is never too early to start planning. All AFA candidates must have excellent grades, be in good physical condition, and exhibit leadership qualities. A guidance counselor or recruiter can suggest extracurricular activities that will enhance an AFA application.

If enlisting seems like a better option, good physical fitness and good grades are still important. ASVAB scores open up more opportunities for any recruit. Be aware that drug use or a criminal record can disqualify an enlistee from service. Enlisted soldiers are also able to seize opportunities to become officers if they exhibit great leadership and ability.

A FUTURE IN THE STARS

Although putting humans in space is difficult and dangerous, in the not-so-distant future, USSF recruits might expect to fly in space or even be stationed there. Commercial space flights are now carrying extremely wealthy individuals and celebrities into space as tourists. The need for security is an unfortunate consequence of any commercial activity.

Many space operations are carried out remotely by machines being controlled from Earth. However, as exploration and other scientific activities move farther away from Earth, it becomes less efficient to react to situations remotely. Machines must transmit data to Earth for a human to analyze, formulate a response, and transmit that response back to be carried out. There will likely be a time when USSF personnel need to be stationed in space to reduce the reaction time to events.

Future projects for the USSF include collaborating on a method of safely reducing or removing the amount of orbital debris in space. A great deal of "space junk" has settled into orbit in the areas of space needed for functioning satellites and spacecraft. It needs to be removed to prevent expensive accidents. Blowing up nonfunctional craft just creates more debris—some of it too tiny to be tracked.

CHUCK YEAGER

General Chuck Yeager (1923–2020) served with the Army Air Corps in World War II. He flew 64 missions over Europe and shot down 13 German planes. Following the war, he became an air force test pilot, and in 1947, he became the first person to break the sound barrier. Due to security concerns, his achievement wasn't announced publicly until 1948.

He continued to test pilot experimental rocket planes, setting numerous records. He was ineligible for the Mercury program despite his many achievements because he didn't have a college degree. In 1962, he became commandant of the Aerospace Research Pilot School at Edwards Air Force Base. There he trained other pilots who would go on to join the astronaut corps—36 were accepted for training and 28 went on to become astronauts. Though he was never accepted for the space program, he piloted many experimental aircraft, including some for NASA.

Yeager's last flight as an active duty air force officer was in 1975. He'd accumulated over 10,000 hours of flight time. In 1976, he was awarded a peacetime Congressional Medal of Honor, presented by President Gerald Ford, and in 1985, he was awarded the Presidential Medal of Freedom by President Reagan. His story is told in Tom Wolfe's *The Right Stuff* and he had a cameo in the 1983 film.

Aerospace manufacturers are also trying to design vehicles with more reusable parts to cut down on the amount of debris left behind.

Developing hypersonic craft is another high-priority project. Lockheed Martin is working with the Department of Defense on this project. Hypersonic craft fly at speeds past Mach 5, which is faster than 3,840 miles (6,180 km) per hour. At those speeds, air friction generates enough heat to melt the fuselage of a standard aircraft, so hypersonic planes have to fly at very high altitudes where the air is colder and thinner. China has been testing hypersonic planes, so this is one of the top priorities for U.S. researchers.

At this time, Great Britain's Royal Air Force is considering forming a space force of its own to protect the country's assets in space. Meanwhile, Russia is consolidating its air and space forces into a single unit. China's space activities are spread out across several agencies. It conducts many launches and test flights, indicating an interest in becoming a power in space.

NASA and SpaceX are collaborating to return humans to the moon. Further exploration of Mars and eventually landing people there is also on the horizon. These projects are likely to require USSF involvement.

The reality is that with so many different nations occupying space now, the United States must protect its assets from destruction or disruption of service. A career in space is not just about what's "out there"—it is about providing safety, security, and services that impact every aspect of daily life. That is why the USSF was created and why the service is a great option for a young tech-savvy person who wants to serve their country.

aerospace Space comprising Earth's atmosphere and the space beyond.

computer virus A computer program that is usually disguised as an innocuous program or file, that often produces copies of itself and inserts them into other programs, and that when run usually performs a malicious action (such as destroying data or damaging software).

cyberspace The online world of computer networks and especially the internet.

engineer A person who is trained in or follows as a profession a branch of engineering.

FORTRAN A computer programming language that resembles algebra in its notation and is widely used for scientific applications.

fuselage The central body portion of an aircraft designed to accommodate the crew and the passengers or cargo.

hypersonic Of or relating to speed five or more times that of sound in air.

launch To release, catapult, or send off (a self-propelled object).

malware Software designed to interfere with a computer's normal functioning.

orbit A path taken by one body in its revolution around another (as by Earth around the sun).

payload The load carried by a vehicle exclusive of what is necessary for its operation.

reveille A bugle call at about sunrise signaling the first military formation of the day.

sound barrier A sudden large increase in aerodynamic drag that occurs as the speed of an aircraft approaches the speed of sound.

surveillance Close watch kept over someone or something.

taps The last bugle call at night blown as a signal that lights are to be put out.

trajectory The curve that a body (such as a planet or comet in its orbit or a rocket) takes in space.

FOR MORE INFORMATION

Air Force ROTC
Website: www.afrotc.com/
The USAF Reserve Officers Training Corp is another path to a military career.

National Aeronautics and Space Administration
300 E Street SW, Suite 5R30
Washington, D.C. 20546
(202) 358-0001
Website: www.nasa.gov/
NASA is the government agency responsible for America's peaceful exploration of space.

The Smithsonian National Air and Space Museum
655 Jefferson Drive SW
Washington, D.C. 20560
(202) 633-2214
Website: airandspace.si.edu/
The National Air and Space Museum is dedicated to preserving the story of man's exploration of the sky. Its collection includes the Wright brothers' 1903 flyer and the prototype space shuttle.

United States Air Force
Website: www.af.mil/
The USAF is the branch of the military dedicated to protecting America's skies.

The United States Air Force Academy Admissions

2304 Cadet Drive, Suite 2400
USAF Academy, CO 80840-5002
(800) 443-9266
rr_admissions@usafa.edu
Website: www.usafa.edu/

The Air Force Academy is a military college that prepares young people for various careers as air force officers.

United States Space Force

Website: www.spaceforce.mil/

The USSF is the newest branch of the military, dedicated to protecting America's interests in space and cyberspace.

Baghchehsara, Ali, Francisco Gallardo Lopez, and Jens Strahmann. *Fundamentals of Aerospace Engineering*. CreateSpace Independent Publishing Platform, 2016.

Browne, Alastair, and Maryann Karinch. *Cosmic Careers: Exploring the Universe of Opportunities in the Space Industries*. New York, NY: HarperCollins, 2021.

Collins, Col. Eileen M., and Jonathan H. Ward. *Through the Glass Ceiling to the Stars: The Story of the First American Woman to Command a Space Mission*. New York, NY: Arcade, 2021.

Gitlin, Marty. *Careers in Personal Space Travel*. Ann Arbor, MI: Cherry Lake Publishing, 2018.

Kaplan Test Prep. *ASVAB Prep Plus 2022–2023: 6 Practice Tests + Proven Strategies + Online + Video*. New York, NY: Kaplan Publishing, 2021.

Kastner, Bernice. *Space Mathematics: Math Problems Based on Space Science*. Newburyport, MA: Dover Publications, 2012.

Keith, Lawrence. *Air Force Enlisted Careers & Job Opportunities: A Guide to Air Force Specialty Codes*. CreateSpace Independent Publishing Platform, 2018.

McCauley, Pamela. *Engineering for Teens: A Beginner's Book for Aspiring Engineers.* Emeryville, CA: Rockridge Press, 2021.

Wildsmith, Snow. *Joining the United States Air Force: A Handbook.* Jefferson, NC: McFarland, 2012.

Wolfe, Tom. *The Right Stuff.* New York, NY: Picador, 1979.

INDEX

Kathleen A. Klatte is the author of several nonfiction books for children and teens. Topics range from animals to constitutional law to even more animals. She lives in New York with one cat and far too many books and Lego.

CREDITS

Designer: Michael Flynn; Editor: Siyavush Saidian